I0447396

# Summary

Passed in 1982, the Nuclear Waste Policy Act (NWPA) was an effort to establish an explicit statutory basis for the Department of Energy (DOE) to dispose of the nation's most highly radioactive nuclear waste. The NWPA requires DOE to remove spent nuclear fuel from commercial nuclear power plants, in exchange for a fee, and transport it to a permanent geologic repository or an interim storage facility before permanent disposal. Defense-related high-level waste is to go into the same repository. In order to achieve this goal, and in an effort to mitigate the political difficulties of imposing a federal nuclear waste facility on a single community, Congress attempted to establish an objective, scientifically based multi-stage statutory process for selecting the eventual site of the nation's new permanent geologic repository. Congress amended the NWPA's site selection process in 1987, however, and designated Yucca Mountain, Nevada, as the sole candidate site for the repository by terminating site specific activities at all other sites.

The Obama Administration, in conjunction with DOE, has taken three important steps directed toward terminating the Yucca Mountain project. First, the Administration's FY2011, FY2012, and FY2013 budget proposals eliminated all funding for the Yucca Mountain project. Second, the President and Secretary of Energy Steven Chu established a Blue Ribbon Commission to consider alternative solutions to the nation's nuclear waste challenge. Third, and most controversial, DOE has attempted to terminate the Nuclear Regulatory Commission's (NRC's) Yucca Mountain licensing proceeding by seeking to withdraw the license application for the Yucca Mountain facility.

DOE's withdrawal motion triggered strong opposition from a number of concerned parties. The states of Washington and South Carolina—each awaiting cleanup and removal of defense-related nuclear waste at the Hanford and Savannah River Sites, respectively—have played significant roles in the legal challenge to the license withdrawal. Claims challenging the Secretary's authority to withdraw the Yucca Mountain license application were filed with both the NRC and the U.S. Court of Appeals for the District of Columbia (D.C. Circuit).

Although DOE's motion to withdraw the Yucca Mountain license application was denied by the NRC's Atomic Safety and Licensing Board, the NRC suspended the Yucca Mountain licensing proceeding in 2011 due to budgetary limitations. The D.C. Circuit has since dismissed a challenge to DOE's authority to withdraw the license application and heard oral arguments on claims challenging NRC's authority to terminate the licensing proceeding.

While the result of the ongoing dispute over the legality of the attempted termination of the Yucca Mountain program remains uncertain, congressional action could have a significant impact on the fate of the Yucca Mountain facility. A number of leading House Republicans have voiced strong opposition to shutting down the Yucca Mountain facility. Consequently, the Yucca Mountain dispute will not only be contested before the NRC and the D.C. Circuit, but also in Congress.

# Contents

# Contacts

# Introduction

Almost 30 years ago, Congress addressed increasing concerns regarding the management of the nation's growing stockpile of nuclear waste by calling for the federal collection of spent nuclear fuel (SNF) and high-level nuclear waste (HLW) for safe, permanent disposal. Passed in 1982, the Nuclear Waste Policy Act (NWPA) was an effort to establish an explicit statutory basis for the Department of Energy (DOE) to dispose of the nation's most highly radioactive nuclear waste. The NWPA requires DOE to remove spent nuclear fuel from commercial nuclear power plants, in exchange for a fee, and transport it to a permanent geologic repository or an interim storage facility before permanent disposal. Defense-related high-level waste is to go into the same repository.[1] In order to achieve this goal, and in an effort to mitigate the political difficulties of imposing a federal nuclear waste facility on a single[2] community, Congress attempted to establish an objective, scientifically based multi-stage statutory process for selecting the eventual site of the nation's new permanent geologic repository.[3] Although DOE would be responsible for developing the eventual repository and carrying out the disposal program, individual nuclear power providers would fund a large portion of the program through significant annual contributions, or fees, to the newly established Nuclear Waste Fund (NWF).[4]

# Establishing a Permanent Geologic Repository for High-Level Nuclear Waste and Spent Nuclear Fuel

The NWPA created a multi-stage statutory framework—requiring the participation of the President, Congress, the Secretary of Energy, the Department of Energy (DOE), and the Nuclear Regulatory Commission (NRC)—that governs the establishment of a permanent geologic nuclear waste repository. The various phases of the process include site recommendation, site characterization and study, site approval, and construction authorization. At the site recommendation stage, the Secretary of Energy (Secretary) was directed to nominate at least five potentially "suitable" sites for an eventual repository.[5] After identifying and conducting an initial study of these sites, the Secretary was to recommend three sites to the President for characterization as "candidate sites."[6] Pursuant to these obligations, the Secretary recommended Deaf Smith County, Texas; Hanford, Washington, and Yucca Mountain, Nevada, to the President in 1986. The Secretary's recommendations were met with significant opposition from the affected states; however, and as a result, Congress amended the NWPA's site selection process in 1987 and designated Yucca Mountain as the sole candidate site for the repository by terminating "all site specific activities (other than reclamation activities) at all candidate sites, other than the Yucca Mountain site."[7] The 1987 amendments, did not, however, end the site characterization, approval,

---

[1] P.L. 97-425, the Nuclear Waste Policy Act (hereinafter NWPA), *codified at* 42 U.S.C. §§10101 *et seq.*

[2] Although the NWPA originally envisioned the construction of a second repository to provide regional balance, the idea was abandoned under the NWPA amendments of 1987.

[3] *NWPA* §§111-125.

[4] *Id.* at §302.

[5] The Secretary nominated sites in Mississippi, Texas, Utah, Washington, and Nevada.

[6] NWPA §112(b).

[7] NWPA §160.

---

and construction authorization phases, which continued as outlined under the original terms of the NWPA.

In accordance with the characterization stage of the NWPA framework, Yucca Mountain was extensively inspected and studied in an effort to determine if the site was in compliance with suitability guidelines established by DOE, and public health, safety, and environmental guidelines established by the Environmental Protection Agency.[8] Following significant litigation over the proper safety standards to be applied to the Yucca Mountain facility, and notwithstanding charges by the state of Nevada that the site was unsafe,[9] Secretary of Energy Spencer Abraham recommended that the President approve the Yucca Mountain site for the development of a repository in 2002.[10] President George W. Bush approved the Yucca Mountain site the next day, and, pursuant to the terms of the NWPA, recommended the site to Congress.

The NWPA, however, provided the state in which the proposed repository would be located with the opportunity to object to the President's site recommendation by submitting a notice of disapproval to Congress.[11] If a notice of disapproval were submitted, the NWPA stated that the site would be "disapproved" unless both houses of Congress overrode the state's objection by passing a "resolution of siting approval."[12] Although Nevada opposed the selection of Yucca Mountain and quickly submitted its notice of disapproval, Congress passed, and the President signed, the necessary approval resolution to override Nevada's objection.[13] Thus, the approval stage of the NWPA process ended.

The fourth stage of the NWPA process commenced in June 2008 when DOE submitted an application for authorization to construct the Yucca Mountain nuclear waste repository (license application) to the NRC. Under the NWPA, "if the President recommends to the Congress the Yucca Mountain site … and the site designation is permitted to take effect … the Secretary shall submit to the [NRC] an application for a construction authorization for a repository at such site."[14] The statute further directed that following submission of the license application, the NRC "shall issue a final decision approving or disapproving the issuance of a construction authorization not later than the expiration of 3 years after the date of the submission of such application."[15] The NRC was considering the 8,600 page license application when the new Obama Administration ushered in a change in policy with respect to the suitability of Yucca Mountain as the future site of the nation's permanent nuclear waste repository.

---

[8] There has been significant litigation over the environmental guidelines to be applied to Yucca Mountain. *See, e.g.*, Nuclear Energy Institute v. EPA, 373 F.3d 1251 (D.C. Cir. 2004).

[9] Two key arguments against Yucca Mountain pertain to the region's overall geologic instability and concerns over water infiltration. *See*, Marta Adams, *Yucca Mountain—Nevada's Perspective*, 46 Idaho L. Rev. 1, 1-6 (2010).

[10] Matthew Wald, *Energy Department Recommends Yucca Mountain for Nuclear Waste Burial*, N.Y. Times, February 15, 2002.

[11] NWPA §115(b).

[12] NWPA §115(c).

[13] P.L. 107-200, 107th Cong. (2002).

[14] NWPA §114(b).

[15] NWPA §114(d).

# Yucca Mountain and the Obama Administration

Both President Obama and Secretary of Energy Steven Chu have stated that Yucca Mountain does not represent a viable option for the permanent storage of nuclear waste.[16] During the 2008 presidential campaign, then-Senator Obama supported Nevada's fight against the repository, asserting in an issue statement on energy policy that he did not believe Yucca Mountain was a "suitable site."[17] In accordance with this view, during his first year in office the Administration requested, and Congress appropriated, only enough funds in FY2010 to continue the NRC license proceeding while halting any design or development progress on the actual repository.[18]

During his second year in office, the President, in conjunction with DOE, took three important steps directed toward terminating the Yucca Mountain facility. First, the Administration's FY2011 budget proposal eliminated all funding for the Yucca Mountain project. Second, the President and Secretary Chu established a Blue Ribbon Commission to consider alternative solutions to the nation's nuclear waste challenge. Third, and most controversially, DOE attempted to terminate the NRC's Yucca Mountain licensing proceeding by seeking to withdraw the license application for the Yucca Mountain facility.

## The Obama Administration Budget

Following years of decreases in program funding going back to the George W. Bush Administration, the Obama Administration and Secretary Chu have resolved to completely defund and terminate the Yucca Mountain program while developing nuclear waste disposal alternatives.[19] DOE's FY2011, FY2012, and FY2013 budget proposals requested no funding for the Yucca Mountain facility. The consecutive budget proposals follow years of steady decreases in funding for the repository: from $572 million in FY2005, to $288 million in FY2009, to only enough funds, approximately $197 million, to finance the ongoing NRC licensing process in FY2010.[20]

### FY2011 Funding

The FY2011 DOE budget request was met with some resistance from both House and Senate appropriators. Senator Patty Murray offered an amendment during the Senate Committee on Appropriations' consideration of the Energy and Water Appropriations bill that would have restored funding to the repository.[21] Similarly, the ranking Member of the House Appropriations Subcommittee on Energy and Water Development, Representative Rodney Frelinghuysen, offered

---

[16] Statement of Steven Chu, Secretary, Department of Energy, Before the Senate Committee on the Budget, March 11, 2009 ("[B]oth the President and I have made clear that Yucca Mountain is not a workable option.").

[17] Obama for America, "Barack Obama and Joe Biden: New Energy for America" (2008), available at http://www.barackobama.com/pdf/factsheet_energy_speech_080308.pdf.

[18] P.L. 111-85, 111th Cong. (2009).

[19] President's FY2011 Budget Proposal at 71, available at http://www.gpoaccess.gov/usbudget/fy11/pdf/budget.pdf.

[20] Statement of Steven Chu, Secretary, Department of Energy, Before the Senate Committee on Appropriations Subcommittee on Energy and Water Development, and Related Agencies, May 19 2009. Secretary Chu had requested $25 million in FY2011 to "wrap up" the Yucca Mountain project and preserve "critical knowledge and data." *See*, Stephen Power, *Chu, Orszag at Odds Over Yucca Funding*, Wall St. J., January 14, 2010.

[21] *Sen. Murray Fails to Revive Nevada Nuke Waste Site*, Seattle Times, July 23, 2010.

an amendment that would have restored $100 million in funding for the Yucca Mountain facility.[22] Both proposals were rejected in committee. Although there was no final action on a full FY2011 budget, Congress passed a series of continuing resolutions that extended appropriations across the federal government "at a rate for operations as provided in the applicable appropriations Acts for fiscal year 2010 and under the authority and conditions provided in such Acts."[23] The final extension, the Department of Defense and Full-Year Continuing Appropriations Act, followed the DOE proposal and provided no funding for the Yucca Mountain program.[24]

In addition to defunding the Yucca Mountain project, the President's FY2011 budget request recommended closing the Office of Civilian Radioactive Waste Management (OCRWM), which had previously been charged with administering the Yucca Mountain project and many of DOE's obligations under the NWPA. After steady reductions in staff the OCRWM officially closed on September 30, 2010.[25] Pursuant to the President's budget proposal, the administration of the NWF and responsibility for DOE's ongoing obligations under the Standard Contract[26] and NWPA have been shifted to the Office of Nuclear Energy.[27] At least two Members of Congress have expressed concern over the legality of the Administration's decision to eliminate the statutorily established OCRWM,[28] which was specifically created by the NWPA for the purpose of "carrying out the functions of the Secretary" under the act.[29]

In response to these concerns, DOE has suggested that the 1977 Department of Energy Organization Act grants the Secretary of Energy "broad authority to create, eliminate, and merge organizations" within DOE.[30] Generally speaking, Congress has the authority to structure the administrative bureaucracy. Thus, absent specific statutory authority, agencies have limited legal power to direct how statutorily defined functions and powers of agencies are to be utilized, allocated, or abandoned.[31] In this instance, the Secretary of Energy has been granted statutory authority to "establish, alter, consolidate or discontinue, such organizational units or components within the Department as he may deem to be necessary or appropriate."[32] The Administration's

---

[22] *House Appropriations Panel Rejects Yucca Mt. Amendment*, Platts, July 16, 2010.

[23] P.L. 111-242, 111th Cong. (2010); P.L. 111-322, 111th Cong. (2010); P.L. 112-4, 112th Cong. (2011).

[24] P.L. 112-10, 112th Cong. (2011).

[25] The OCRWM workforce at Yucca Mountain consisted of as many as 2,700 employees. DOE has stated that it will help employees "find new opportunities, including working to help employees find new positions in the department and throughout the federal government through career transition programs." Emily Yehle, *Yucca Project's Last 600 Employees Scramble for New Jobs*, N.Y. Times, August 4, 2010.

[26] Under the NWPA, DOE was authorized to enter into contracts with private nuclear facilities to allow the federal government to take possession of nuclear waste and ensure its storage and disposal in a prospective permanent geologic repository. In an effort to streamline the collection and disposal process, DOE elected to create a single "Standard Contract for Disposal of Spent Nuclear Fuel and/or High Level Radioactive Waste" for use with nuclear power providers. For additional information on the government's obligations under the Standard Contract, see CRS Report R40996, *Contract Liability Arising from the Nuclear Waste Policy Act (NWPA) of 1982*, by Todd Garvey.

[27] President's FY2011 Budget Proposal, at 71.

[28] *See*, Letter from Congressman Ralph Hall and Congressman Paul Broun, to Steven Chu, Secretary of Energy, February 3, 2010.

[29] 42 U.S.C. §10224 ("There hereby is established within the Department of Energy an Office of Civilian Radioactive Waste Management.").

[30] P.L. 95-91, 95th Cong. (1977); Janice Valverde, *Two House Republicans Challenge Decision to End Yucca Mountain Funding, Close Office*, BNA Daily Report for Executives, February 9, 2010.

[31] *See, e.g.,* Kendall v. U.S. ex. rel Stokes, 37 U.S. (12 Pet.) 524 (1838)(holding that the President has no authority to direct the Post Master's performance of his statutory duty).

[32] 42 U.S.C. §7253.

proposal—which Congress, through its appropriation power, is free to either follow or disregard—is to "terminate" the OCRWM and transfer the office's responsibilities to the Office of Nuclear Energy.[33] Given the Secretary's statutorily granted authority, it is likely that such a transfer would be a valid consolidation of DOE offices. However, any statutory duties or obligations that were placed in OCRWM must continue to be carried out by the Office of Nuclear Energy.[34]

## FY2012 Funding

Like the FY2011 budget proposal, DOE's FY2012 budget proposal again requested no funding for the Yucca Mountain program. As a result of growing opposition from its Members, the House rejected DOE's proposal and passed an appropriations bill that included $25 million for DOE to continue work on the program.[35] The Senate, however, opposed the provision, and ultimately no funding for the Yucca Mountain program was included in the final Consolidated Appropriations Act of 2012.[36] With no funding for the program in the FY2012 enacted appropriations, Congress as a whole has not appropriated funds for Yucca Mountain activities since FY2010. As a result, DOE completed its shutdown of the Yucca Mountain facility.

## FY2013 Funding

The Administration's FY2013 budget request again included no funding for the Yucca Mountain facility, but the House of Representatives appears to again be attempting to return funding to the project.[37] On April 25, 2012, the House Committee on Appropriations voted to include $25 million in the Energy and Water Development Appropriations bill "to continue the [DOE's] congressionally-mandated activities to continue the Yucca Mountain license application activity."[38] The version of the bill approved by the Senate Appropriations Committee included no such funding, but did include language directing DOE to implement a pilot program for the operation of "consolidated storage facilities."[39]

# Blue Ribbon Commission on America's Nuclear Future

Shortly before releasing the FY2011 budget proposal, the President asked DOE to establish the Blue Ribbon Commission on America's Nuclear Future (Commission) to explore, study, and evaluate alternatives to the Yucca Mountain facility for the permanent storage of SNF.[40] The 15-member Commission, appointed by the Secretary of Energy, consists of distinguished scientists,

---

[33] Department of Energy FY2011 Congressional Budget Request at 176 (February 2010) ("The Administration has ... decided to terminate the Office of Civilian Radioactive Waste Management.").

[34] Such duties include annually preparing and submitting to Congress a "comprehensive report on the activities and expenditures of the office." 42 U.S.C. §10224.

[35] H.R. 2354, 112th Cong. (2011).

[36] P.L. 112-74, 112th Cong. (2011).

[37] *See*, FY2013 DOE Budget Request to Congress, available at http://www.cfo.doe.gov/budget/13budget/index13 html.

[38] H.R. 5325, 112th Cong. (2012); H.Rept. 112-462, 112th Cong. (2012) at 108.

[39] S. 2465, 112th Cong. (2012); S.Rept. 112-164, 112th Cong. (2012) at 78.

[40] Memorandum from President Barack Obama, to Steven Chu, Secretary of Energy, *Blue Ribbon Commission on America's Nuclear Future*, January 29, 2010.

---

academics, industry representatives, labor representatives, and former elected officials.[41] The Commission's goal is to "provide recommendations for developing a safe, long-term solution to managing the nation's used nuclear fuel and nuclear waste."[42] The Commission would not, however, consider specific sites for a future repository.[43]

Co-chaired by former Congressman Lee Hamilton and former National Security Advisor Brent Scowcroft, the Commission was charged with producing an interim report within 18 months of the Commission's establishment and a final report within 24 months.[44] Although not expressly prohibited from considering Yucca Mountain as a potential solution to the nation's nuclear waste problems,[45] Secretary Chu and the White House conveyed that the Commission was to focus only on "alternatives" to Yucca Mountain. Accordingly, the Commission co-chairs stated that "Secretary Chu has made it quite clear that nuclear waste storage at Yucca Mountain is not an option."[46] In a February 11, 2011, letter to Co-chairs Hamilton and Scowcroft, Secretary Chu reaffirmed that the Commission should not consider Yucca Mountain as a viable nuclear waste disposal solution. In the letter, Secretary Chu reiterated that it was time to "turn the page and look for a better solution—one that is not only scientifically sound but that also can achieve a greater level of public acceptance than would have been possible at Yucca Mountain. It is time to move beyond the 25 year old stalemate over Yucca Mountain."[47]

The Commission issued its final report on January 26, 2012.[48] As expected, the report did not make any specific recommendations as to the "suitability" of Yucca Mountain, other than to make clear that the process of selecting and establishing the Yucca Mountain facility has suffered from several flaws and should be replaced by a new "consent-based approach" that provides "incentives" and encourages interested communities to "volunteer" as a potential host site for an eventual repository.[49] While acknowledging that "the future of the Yucca Mountain project

---

[41] A list of Commission members is available at http://brc.gov/members html.

[42] DOE Press Release, *Secretary Chu Announces Blue Ribbon Commission on America's Nuclear Future*, January 29, 2010. Available at http://www.doe.gov. According to Secretary Chu, the Commission will be looking at "different types of disposal options." Janice Valverde, *Administration to Withdraw License Bid for Yucca Mountain, Eliminates Funding*, BNA Daily Report for Executives, February 2, 2010.

[43] DOE itself is currently prohibited by statute from considering specific sites other than Yucca Mountain. 42 U.S.C. §10172 ("The Secretary shall terminate all site specific activities ... at all candidate sites, other than the Yucca Mountain site, within 90 days after the enactment of the Nuclear Waste Policy Amendments Act of 1987.").

[44] The Commission held its first meeting on March 25 and 26, 2010. The Commission is divided into three sub-committees focusing on disposal, reactor fuel cycle technology, and transportation and storage. For updated information on the Commission's work see http://brc.gov.

[45] The initial House-passed bill approving the Administration's FY2010 proposed budget included language mandating that any review of nuclear waste disposal alternatives include Yucca Mountain as a potential option. However, the final DOE appropriations bill contained language mandating only that DOE "consider all alternatives for nuclear waste disposal." P.L. 111-85 (2009).

[46] Steve Tetreault, *Federal Panel to Examine Nuclear Waste Storage*, Las Vegas Review-Journal, January 30, 2010. *But cf.*, Memorandum and Order, Atomic Safety and Licensing Board, Docket No. 63-001-HLW, June 29, 2010, at 19 n.69 ("There appears to be no express contradiction of the House Report language, which requires the Blue Ribbon Commission to consider Yucca Mountain, in either the Conference Report or the Senate Report and thus the language in the House Report appears to be the law.").

[47] Letter from Steven Chu, Secretary of Energy, to Lee Hamilton and Brent Scowcroft, Co-Chairs, Blue Ribbon Commission on America's Nuclear Future, February 11, 2011, available at http://brc.gov/library/correspondence/BRC_Letter_from_Secretary_Chu_2-11-2011.pdf.

[48] Final Report to the Secretary of Energy, Blue Ribbon Commission on America's Nuclear Future (January 26, 2012). *Available at* http://brc.gov/sites/default/files/documents/brc_finalreport_jan2012.pdf.

[49] *Id.* at ix.

---

remains uncertain," the Commission did make specific findings that may have significant influence over the future of nuclear waste disposal.[50] Importantly, the Commission concluded that deep geologic disposal "is the most promising and accepted method [of disposal] currently available," and therefore recommended that the United States "should undertake an integrated nuclear waste management program that leads to the timely development of one or more permanent deep geological facilities for the safe disposal of spent fuel and high-level nuclear waste."[51] Additionally, the Commission concluded that "new institutional leadership for the nation's nuclear waste program is clearly needed."[52] The final report therefore recommended that control over nuclear waste disposal be removed from DOE, and instead vested in a newly established "single-purpose organization" that could "provide the stability, focus, and credibility that are essential to get the waste program back on track."[53] The Commission found a sufficiently independent "federal corporation chartered by Congress" to be the most promising structure for this new entity.[54] Finally, the Commission reiterated the severe consequences of continued delays and urged Congress and the President to take action to institute the Commission's recommendations "without further delay."[55]

Congress has thus far taken no action to implement the BRC recommendations.

## Attempted Withdrawal of the Yucca Mountain Construction Authorization License

The most controversial action taken by DOE has been the agency's attempted withdrawal of the Yucca Mountain license application in an effort to terminate the NRC's ongoing licensing proceeding. DOE has made clear that the decision to withdraw the license, initially submitted in June 2008,[56] was based on "policy" considerations.[57] Specifically, DOE has asserted that scientific and technological advancements since the enactment of the NWPA, such as dry cask storage and advanced recycling, "provide an opportunity to develop better alternatives to Yucca Mountain."[58] Although the NRC's Atomic Safety and Licensing Board rejected DOE's attempt to withdraw the

---

[50] *Id.* at 23.

[51] *Id.* at 29. The Commission thus recommended the same general form of disposal as was planned at the Yucca Mountain facility.

[52] *Id.* at 60.

[53] *Id.* at x.

[54] *Id.* at 61.

[55] *Id.* at xv.

[56] The NRC reportedly spent $58 million in FY2009 to review the Yucca Mountain license. *See,* Janice Valverde, *Administration to Withdraw License Bid for Yucca Mountain, Eliminates Funding,* BNA Daily Report for Executives, February 2, 2010.

[57] *See,* Nuclear Regulatory Commission Atomic Safety and Licensing Board, Memorandum and Order, *In the Matter of U.S. Department of Energy,* ASLBP No. 09-892-HLW-CAB04 (June 29, 2010) at 2 ("Conceding that the Application is not flawed nor the site unsafe, the Secretary of Energy seeks to withdraw the Application with prejudice as a 'matter of policy' because the Nevada site 'is not a workable option.'") *See also,* Nuclear Regulatory Commission Atomic Safety and Licensing Board, U.S. Department of Energy's Reply to the Responses to the Motion to Withdraw, *In the Matter of U.S. Department of Energy,* ASLBP No. 09-892-HLW-CAB04 (May 27, 2010) at 1 (Characterizing the question presented as whether the Secretary has authority "to seek withdrawal of a license application for a repository when the Secretary has determined, as a matter of policy, not to proceed with that repository.").

[58] *See,* Brief for Respondents, In re Aiken County, No. 10-1050 (D.C. Cir. January 3, 2011). DOE has also cited consistent opposition from Nevada as a reason for the policy shift.

---

license—a decision that the NRC has not reversed—the license review proceedings have been suspended pursuant to budget constraints.[59]

DOE formally filed its motion asking the Atomic Safety and Licensing Board (Board) to dismiss the application "with prejudice" on March 3, 2010.[60] A common legal term, an application that is withdrawn "with prejudice" is generally barred from being refiled in the future. However, whether or not an application, motion, or claim is dismissed with prejudice is a decision made by the Board and the NRC, and not by the requesting party.[61] DOE specifically asked the Board to dismiss the application with prejudice because the agency "does not intend ever to refile an application to construct a permanent geologic repository for spent nuclear fuel and high-level radioactive waste at Yucca Mountain."[62] As construction on the Yucca Mountain facility cannot continue without a construction authorization from the NRC, many commentators consider a successful "with prejudice" withdrawal as marking the formal termination of any potential repository at Yucca Mountain.[63]

DOE's withdrawal motion triggered strong opposition from a number of concerned parties. The states of Washington and South Carolina—each awaiting cleanup and removal of defense-related nuclear waste at the Hanford and Savannah River Sites, respectively—have led the legal challenge against the license withdrawal.[64] Similar legal claims[65] were immediately filed in two different venues. Washington; South Carolina; Aiken County, South Carolina; the Prairie Island Indian Community; and the National Association of Regulatory and Utility Commissioners (NARUC) petitioned to intervene in the NRC licensing proceeding in order to stop the withdrawal. Washington, South Carolina, and Aiken County, along with a group of private plaintiffs from Washington State, have also filed statutory claims in the D.C. Circuit challenging DOE's authority[66] to withdraw the license application.[67]

---

[59] *See*, "NRC Suspends Licensing Proceedings."

[60] U.S. Department of Energy's Motion to Withdraw, *In the Matter of U.S. Department of Energy*, ASLBP No. 09-892-HLW-CAB04, March 3, 2010.

[61] 10 C.F.R. §2.107 ("The Commission may ... on receiving a request for withdrawal of an application, deny the application or dismiss it with prejudice."). Under NRC procedures, decisions by the Board are appealable to the Commission as a whole.

[62] U.S. Department of Energy's Motion to Withdraw, *In the Matter of U.S. Department of Energy*, ASLBP No. 09-892-HLW-CAB04, March 3, 2010.

[63] *See*, 42. U.S.C. §10134; Shannon Dininny, *Wash. to Intervene in Yucca Mountain Case*, Seattle Times, March 1 2010. If the application were dismissed with prejudice, it is an open question as to whether the application could then be refiled at a later date by a different agency.

[64] The nuclear waste located at the Hanford and the Savannah River sites was intended for disposal at Yucca Mountain.

[65] The arguments made before the NRC and the D.C. Circuit were essentially the same, with the core arguments focusing on the NWPA, the National Environmental Policy Act, and the Administrative Procedure Act.

[66] NARUC also filed a case with the D.C. Circuit to bar the Secretary from collecting Nuclear Waste Fund fees. *See*, National Association of Regulatory Utility Commissioners v. DOE, 2010 U.S. App. LEXIS 25579 (D.C. Cir. December 13, 2010).

[67] It is important to recognize that the litigation associated with DOE's attempts to withdraw the license application is distinct from the contract litigation currently proceeding in the U.S. Court of Federal Claims and the U.S. Court of Appeals for the Federal Circuit. The contract claims seek damages based on a partial breach of the Standard Contract entered into by DOE and individual nuclear power providers, whereas the claims before the NRC and the D.C. Circuit are asking those bodies to prohibit the Secretary of Energy from withdrawing the Yucca Mountain license application. The license withdrawal decision may have an impact on future liability in the contract cases in as far as it leads to further delays in DOE's ability to begin collecting and disposing of nuclear waste covered under the Standard Contract. For more information on the contract claims, see CRS Report R40996, *Contract Liability Arising from the Nuclear* (continued...)

The legal battle over the Secretary's authority to withdraw the license application hinges on specific statutory language within the NWPA. Section 114 outlines the process for obtaining the necessary site approval and construction authorization and provides the statutory foundation for the ongoing litigation.[68] The provision states that once the site approval procedures are completed and the site is designated, as was the case with Yucca Mountain, "the Secretary *shall* submit to the [NRC] an application for a construction authorization for a repository."[69] Upon submission of the application, the NRC "*shall* consider" the application "in accordance with the laws applicable to such applications, except that the [NRC] *shall* issue a final decision approving or disapproving the issuance of a construction authorization not later than the expiration of 3 years after the date of the submission of such application."[70]

DOE has put forth three main arguments in support of the agency's motion to withdraw the license application. First, at a general level, DOE argues that the Secretary's decision to withdraw the license application, a decision the agency characterizes as a "discretionary" policy choice, should be granted significant deference by both the NRC and the federal courts.[71] The Secretary, and the President, clearly have broad discretion in carrying out the procedures outlined by the NWPA for establishing a permanent geologic repository.[72] For example, the Secretary exercises broad discretion under the NWPA both before and after the licensing process. Most starkly, Section 113 states: "[i]f the Secretary at anytime determines the Yucca Mountain site to be unsuitable for development as a repository, the Secretary shall ... terminate all site characterization activities at such site."[73] This provision gives the Secretary broad authority to terminate the Yucca Mountain program "at any time" as long as he finds the site "unsuitable." However, the authority found in Section 113, entitled "Site Characterization,"[74] presumably applies only during the site characterization phase—a phase terminated once the Secretary recommended Yucca Mountain to the President. Whether the Secretary retains discretion during the license application phase, as governed by the explicit language of Section 114, is a key question to be resolved by the NRC and the D.C. Circuit.

Second, DOE has argued that the NWPA specifically incorporates NRC regulations that allow for the withdrawal of a license application by ensuring that that license application be considered in accordance "with the laws applicable to such applications."[75] The laws applicable to NRC license applications would include general procedural regulations promulgated by the NRC.[76] These regulations clearly recognize the ability of an applicant to request the withdrawal of a license

---

(...continued)

*Waste Policy Act (NWPA) of 1982*, by Todd Garvey.

[68] NWPA §114.

[69] NWPA §114(b) (emphasis added).

[70] NWPA §114(d) (emphasis added).

[71] U.S. Department of Energy's Motion to Withdraw, *In the Matter of U.S. Department of Energy*, ASLBP No. 09-892-HLW-CAB04 (March 3, 2010).

[72] *See*, NWPA §§112-113.

[73] NWPA §113.

[74] As noted previously the NWPA sets up what amounts to a four-phase program for establishing a permanent repository. These phases are entitled characterization, recommendation, approval, and authorization. *See*, NWPA §§112-115.

[75] U.S. Department of Energy's Motion to Withdraw, *In the Matter of U.S. Department of Energy*, ASLBP No. 09-892-HLW-CAB04 (March 3, 2010) at 5.

[76] *See*, 10 C.F.R. Part 2.

---

application from consideration before the NRC or the Board.[77] Thus, because the NWPA seems to incorporate "applicable" NRC regulations, DOE has asserted that the NWPA's requirement that the Secretary submit the application must be read in conjunction with NRC regulations that allow withdrawal.[78] Under such a reading, the NWPA could be interpreted to express Congress's clear intent that, following the submission of the license application, any license proceeding must progress subject to existing NRC procedural regulations.

Finally, DOE has argued that even if Section 114 required that the Secretary submit the license application, nothing in the statute restricts the Secretary's actions after the application is submitted.[79] Under DOE's interpretation of the statute, the agency's statutory obligations with regard to the license application were satisfied in June 2008 when the agency formally submitted the license application. What the Secretary chooses to do with the application after submission is viewed by DOE as outside the scope of Section 114's language.

Those who oppose DOE's authority to withdraw the license application rely on the plain language of Section 114. The challengers take the position that the Secretary's interpretation of Section 114 would essentially "render the [provision's] plain language meaningless."[80] Pursuant to this position, the challengers argue that the NWPA clearly expressed Congress's intent that the license proceeding be carried through to its ultimate conclusion. Section 114 states that the Secretary "shall" submit the license application to the NRC and that the NRC "shall" not only consider the application, but also issue a final decision within a three-year time frame.[81] In conjunction with the requirement that the Secretary provide Congress with status reports on the progress of the license application,[82] the challengers interpret these provisions as Congress's attempt to mandate that DOE initiate the licensing proceeding by filing the application, at which point authority over the application transfers to the NRC to subsequently carry out its obligation to reach a final decision. Ultimately, the challengers view the NWPA as creating a step-by-step process, complete with reporting obligations, that necessarily leads to a final decision on the merits of the license application by the NRC.[83] Challengers argue that a DOE interpretation that would allow the Secretary to terminate the license proceeding prior to the NRC's final determination would be contrary to Congress's clear intent.

## NRC Administrative Proceedings

The Board, which had been reviewing the Yucca Mountain license application since the application was submitted in June of 2008, is an "independent trial-level adjudicatory body" that conducts all licensing hearings for the NRC.[84] The Board generally consists of three administrative judges, but unlike other administrative adjudicative bodies, not all Board judges

---

[77] 10 C.F.R. §2.107. Although this provision authorizes a party to request withdrawal, it is unlikely that the provision establishes a right to withdrawal.

[78] U.S. Department of Energy Motion to Withdraw, *In the Matter of U.S Department of Energy*, ASLBP No. 09-892-HLW-CAB04, (March 3, 2010).

[79] *Id.* at 5-6.

[80] *See, e.g.,* Motion for Preliminary Injunction, Washington v. DOE, No-10-1050 (D.C. Cir. April 13, 2010) at 11.

[81] NWPA §114(b); NWPA §114(d).

[82] NWPA §114(c).

[83] *See, e.g.,* Motion for Preliminary Injunction, Washington v. DOE, No-10-1050 (D.C. Cir. April 13, 2010).

[84] *Nuclear Regulatory Commission: ASLBP Responsibilities*, available at http://www.nrc.gov/about-nrc/regulatory/adjudicatory/aslbp-respons html.

are trained lawyers. A given panel generally consists of a mix of legal and technical judges.[85] Technical judges must be "persons of recognized caliber and stature in the nuclear field" and generally have substantial experience in nuclear engineering.[86]

DOE filed its motion to withdraw the Yucca Mountain license application with the Board on March 3, 2010. On April 6, 2010, the Board issued an initial opinion questioning its own authority to adjudicate the dispute while noting that many of the significant legal questions involved with DOE's motion to withdraw were currently pending before the D.C. Circuit.[87] Given the circumstances, the Board decided to avoid reaching the merits of DOE's withdrawal motion and, "in the interest of judicial efficiency," suspended consideration of DOE's motion "pending guidance from the Court of Appeals on the relevant legal issues."[88]

The Board's decision was immediately appealed by DOE to the full NRC, where the Commission overturned the order.[89] Asserting that the independent agency had a significant role to play in the ongoing legal dispute, the NRC reminded the Board that "the application of our expertise in the interpretation of the [Atomic Energy Act], the NWPA, and our own regulations will, at a minimum, inform the court in the consideration of the issues raised by DOE's motion to withdraw."[90] Additionally, the NRC noted that it was unclear when, or even if, the D.C. Circuit would provide the guidance sought by the Board given questions as to whether the D.C. Circuit had jurisdiction to reach the merits of the Yucca Mountain claims before it.[91] Therefore, rather than rely on a determination by the D.C. Circuit, the NRC remanded the case to the Board to "resolve the matter pending before our agency as expeditiously and responsibly as possible."[92]

The NRC's rebuke of the Board's order was not surprising given the traditional roles of administrative adjudicatory bodies and federal courts. Generally speaking, where similar claims are simultaneously filed before an agency and a federal court, the court, for reasons of judicial efficiency, will typically allow the administrative proceeding to reach an independent conclusion rather than simultaneously consider the same questions.[93] In this way the federal court allows the parties the opportunity to resolve their claims at the administrative level, and allows the agency to establish a factual record upon which, on a potential appeal, the federal court can base its own legal conclusions. Additionally, by allowing the agency to reach an initial decision, the federal court receives the benefit of the agency's subject-matter expertise.[94] Consistent with this

---

[85] *Id.*

[86] *Nuclear Regulatory Commission: Atomic Safety and Licensing Board Panel*, available at http://www.nrc.gov/about-nrc/organization/aslbpfuncdesc.html.

[87] As previously noted, claims opposing DOE's withdrawal were simultaneously filed with the NRC and the D.C. Circuit.

[88] Memorandum and Order, *In the Matter of U.S. Department of Energy*, ASLBP No. 09-892-HLW-CAB04 (April 6, 2010) at 3.

[89] Memorandum and Order, *In the Matter of U.S. Department of Energy*, No. 63-001-HLW (April 23, 2010).

[90] *Id.* at 4.

[91] For example, judicial review is generally limited to "final agency action." However, the NWPA provides the D.C. Circuit with jurisdiction over any claim "alleging the failure of the Secretary, the President, or the Commission to make any decision, or take any action, required under this subtitle ..." NWPA §119(a).

[92] Memorandum and Order, *In the Matter of U.S. Department of Energy*, No. 63-001-HLW (April 23, 2010) at 4.

[93] This general practice is based on the APA's requirement of "finality" and the general requirement that a party exhaust the available administrative process before bringing a claim to federal court. *See*, 5 U.S.C. §704; McGee v. United States, 402 U.S. 479 (1971).

[94] *See, e.g.,* Memorandum and Order, *In the Matter of U.S. Department of Energy*, No. 63-001-HLW (April 23, 2010) (continued...)

---

traditional allocation of duties, the D.C. Circuit, rather than taking up the claims as the Board had hoped, released an order delaying its consideration of the Yucca Mountain claims until the NRC's evaluation of DOE's motion was complete.[95]

## *Ruling of the Atomic Safety and Licensing Board*

Ordered by the NRC to reach a final decision on DOE's motion, the Board responded with a sweeping opinion ruling that Secretary Chu did not have the authority to withdraw the Yucca Mountain license application.[96] The Board rejected the discretion that DOE had argued for, concluding instead that the statutory language of the NWPA "mandates progress towards a merits decision," which DOE could not "single handedly derail" by withdrawing the license application.[97] Beginning with the plain language of Section 114, the Board held that Congress had established a "detailed, specific procedure" that removed control of the license application process from the Secretary by creating a mandatory statutory scheme.[98] Under this scheme, the official site designation triggered DOE's obligation to submit the license application, which once submitted, in turn triggered a "duty on NRC's part to consider and to render a decision on the application."[99] In the Board's view, to allow DOE to withdraw the application as a matter of policy at this stage would be contrary to Congress's intent that the licensing process be "removed from the political process."[100] Drawing a distinction between the clearly discretionary site characterization phase detailed in Section 113, and the mandatory language of Section 114, the Board noted that "[c]learly, when Congress wished to permit DOE to terminate activities, it knew how to do so."[101] With no such inclusion of discretionary language in Section 114, the Board denied the Secretary's authority to withdraw the license application.

The Board also rejected DOE's argument that the NWPA reflected Congress's intent to integrate NRC procedural regulations that allow for withdrawal. First, the Board characterized 10 C.F.R. Section 2.107 as a clarification of the NRC's authority to grant or deny a motion for withdrawal, rather than a "presumptive" grant of permission to an applicant to "unilaterally withdraw [an] application."[102] Additionally, the Board concluded that Congress would not obliquely alter a "fundamental" aspect of the NWPA's licensing scheme through "vague terms or ancillary provisions."[103] "It would require a strained and tortured reading of the NWPA," held the Board, "to conclude that Congress intended that its explicit mandate to the NRC ... might be nullified by a nonspecific reference to an obscure NRC procedural regulation."[104]

---

(...continued)

at 4.

[95] Per Curiam Order, *In re Aiken County*, No. 10-1050 (D.C. Cir. July 28, 2010).

[96] Memorandum and Order, *In the Matter of U.S. Department of Energy*, ASLBP No. 09-892-HLW-CAB04 (June 29, 2010) (hereinafter ASLB Order).

[97] *Id.* at 3.

[98] *Id.* at 6.

[99] *Id.* at 7.

[100] *Id.* at 9.

[101] *Id.* at 8.

[102] *Id.* at 13.

[103] *Id.* at 14.

[104] *Id.*

In reaching its conclusion, the Board also gave significant weight to Congress's 2002 decision to override Nevada's objection to establishing the future repository at Yucca Mountain. As previously noted, once President Bush designated Yucca Mountain as the candidate site for the nation's permanent repository and recommended the site to Congress, under Section 115 and Section 116 of the NWPA Nevada was authorized to veto that designation by submitting to Congress a notice of disapproval.[105] However, the NWPA permits Congress to override the state's objection by passing a resolution approving of the site. In accordance with these procedures, Nevada submitted a notice of disapproval, which Congress then overrode in P.L. 107-200. The Board interpreted this as reserving to Congress the ultimate decision "as to whether the Yucca Mountain project was to move forward."[106] The Board reasoned that "by overruling Nevada's disapproval of the Yucca Mountain site Congress was commanding, as a matter of policy, that Yucca Mountain was to move forward" with the license application to be decided on its "technical merits" by the NRC.[107]

Although DOE's motion was denied outright, the Board went on to state in dicta that, even were a withdrawal of the application permitted, the dismissal should not be granted "with prejudice." The Board noted that NRC practice has traditionally reserved "with prejudice" dismissals for situations in which the Board has reached the merits of the application.[108] With the Board having reached no merits-based decision on any aspect of the license application, any dismissal should, according to the Board, be without prejudice. Additionally, the Board determined that the "public interest" would not be served if the current Secretary's judgment on Yucca Mountain could "tie the hands of future administrations for all time."[109]

## NRC Appeal and Suspension of the Licensing Proceeding

One day after the Board's decision, and before DOE filed a formal appeal, the NRC released an order inviting the parties to file briefs on whether the Commission should review the Board's decision.[110] By the fall of 2010, the parties had filed all briefs, all Commissioners had cast their votes, and a final order from the NRC was expected at any moment.[111] Yet, a final decision was not issued until September 2011. Some Members of Congress accused Chairman Jaczko of delaying the NRC decision by "footdragging."[112] However, in testimony before the House

---

[105] NWPA §§115-116.

[106] *ASLB Order*, at 10. Although the Board gave the congressional approval resolution great weight, it is important to note that had Nevada not objected to the designation of the Yucca Mountain site, no approval resolution would have been necessary for the Yucca Mountain project to move forward. The purpose of the resolution was simply to override Nevada's objection.

[107] *Id.*

[108] *Id.* at 21-22

[109] *Id.* at 21.

[110] Order of the Nuclear Regulatory Commission, *In the Matter of U.S. Department of Energy*, No. 63-001-HLW (June 30, 2010).

[111] Commissioner Svinicki voted on August 25, 2010; Chairman Jaczko initially voted on August 25 as well, but withdrew his vote on August 30, and submitted his final vote on October 29, 2010; Commissioner Ostendorff voted on August 26, 2010; and Commissioner Magwood voted on September 15, 2010. *See*, Report of Hubert T. Bell, Inspector General, Nuclear Regulatory Commission, *NRC Chairman's Unilateral Decision to Terminate NRC's Review of DOE Yucca Mountain Repository License Application*, OIG Case No. 11-05. *Available at* http://republicans.energycommerce house.gov/Media/file/Hearings/Environment/061411/IGREPORT.PDF (hereinafter *NRC IG Report*).

[112] *See*, The Role of the Nuclear Regulatory Commission in America's Energy Future: Hearing Before the H. (continued...)

---

Subcommittee on Energy and Power and Subcommittee on Environment and the Economy, Chairman Jaczko stated that the Commission could not move from what he characterized as "preliminary views" to a final order without a "majority position."[113] Pursuant to NRC voting guidelines,[114] when considering a matter, Commissioners will initially circulate votes along with explanations of their positions. Once a majority position is reached, the Commission then holds a public affirmation session and issues a final order.[115] Although all Commissioners had issued preliminary votes and a draft order had been before the Commission since November 1, 2010, the Commissioners were apparently unable to agree on a majority position to be articulated in the final order.[116]

## NRC Halts License Review Through Budget Guidance

Although the appeal was still pending before the NRC, controversy over the Yucca Mountain license application intensified in October 2010 when NRC Chairman Gregory Jaczko directed NRC staff to use funds appropriated under the FY2011 Continuing Appropriations Act (CR) to close down the agency's review of the Yucca Mountain license application.[117] As noted

---

(...continued)

Subcommittee on Energy and Power and the Subcommittee on Environment and the Economy, 112th Cong. (May 4, 2011); Steve Tetreault, "Vote Timing Nettles Repository Backers," *Las Vegas Review Journal* (November 10, 2010). There has also been controversy regarding NRC's ability to render a fair and objective decision on DOE's license withdrawal.[112] The NRC consists of five commissioners, three of whom—William Magwood, William Ostendorff, and George Apostolakis—were nominated by President Obama and confirmed by the Senate in February 2010. During the Senate confirmation hearing for the three nominees, Sen. Barbara Boxer specifically asked each nominee whether, as commissioners, they would "second guess [DOE's] decision to withdraw the license application for Yucca Mountain from NRC's review." All three responded "No." Hearing before the Senate Committee on Environment and Public Works, February 11, 2010. As a result, Aiken County filed a motion with the NRC accusing the commissioners in question of having an improper predisposition for overturning the Board's decision and asking that all three commissioners recuse themselves from the NRC's review. *Aiken County Response in Opposition to Commission Review of ASLB Order*, Docket No. 63-001-HLW, ASLBP No. 09-892-HLW-CAB04, July 8, 2010. Although none of the commissioners recused themselves in response to the motion by Aiken County, Commissioner Apostolakis did recuse himself from the appeal because he had previously been involved with an independent assessment of the Yucca Mountain license.

[113] *Id.*

[114] NRC Voting guidelines are nonbinding and are not consistently followed. *See*, *NRC IG Report*, *supra* note 111, at 45.

[115] *See*, NRC Internal Commission Procedures, Chapter III: Voting. *Available at* http://www.nrc.gov/about-nrc/policy-making/internal html.

[116] Under NRC procedures, Commission action requires majority approval. *Id.* ("A majority Commission position is needed for action."). Thus, as the voting guidelines expressly state: "requests for Commission action will be denied if the Commission vote is 2-2. Therefore, a 2-2 vote will result in: … denial of review of Licensing Board decisions." *Id.* at App. 5. During the period between the fall of 2010 and the fall of 2011, Chairman Jaczko had taken the position that until there was a majority position among the Commissioners, the Board's decision could neither be affirmed nor reversed, and therefore would remain in limbo until consensus could be reached among the four participating Commissioners. At least one Commissioner adopted the opposite position—citing NRC voting procedures—that absent a majority position, the Board's decision should be upheld. According to the *NRC IG Report*, "Commissioner Ostendorff concluded that based on the Internal Commission Procedures, a 2-2 voting split would uphold the ASLB's decision." *NRC IG Report*, *supra* note 111 at 36. The NRC Inspector General investigation highlighted the ambiguous nature of the NRC voting procedures, finding that the "written procedures do not provide details on the process that occurs between the completion of a … vote and the conduct of an affirmation vote on the matter. The lack of enforcement of and specificity in the Commission's written procedures … allows matters to sit in abeyance without final Commission action." *Id.* at 45.

[117] Memorandum to Office Directors and Regional Administrators from J.E. Dyer, Chief Financial Officer, Nuclear Regulatory Commission, *Guidance Under A Fiscal Year 2011 Continuing Resolution* (October 4 2010) (hereinafter (continued...)

---

previously, Congress passed a series of CRs to extend FY2011 appropriations across the federal government "at a rate for operations as provided in the applicable appropriations Acts for fiscal year 2010 and under the authority and conditions provided in such Acts."[118] In an October 4, 2010, memorandum, NRC staff were instructed to continue their Yucca Mountain activities "in accordance with the Commission's decisions on the FY 2011 budget using available Nuclear Waste Fund resources during the CR."[119] Thus, NRC staff were directed to follow the agency's FY2011 budget request rather than enacted FY2010 appropriations. Noting that the Senate Appropriations Committee and the House Appropriations Energy and Water Development Subcommittee had approved the NRC's 2011 budget request, Chairman Jaczko justified the budget guidance as "consistent with NRC's obligation to spend funds prudently under a Continuing Resolution pending final budget by the Congress."[120] Although Chairman Jaczko had suggested that a closure of NRC license review activities would include the Board's license review, the Board initially denied a DOE motion to stay the licensing proceedings and expressed a desire to "move this proceeding forward as expeditiously as circumstances permit."[121]

The NRC's FY2011 budget request, which anticipated DOE's attempt to withdraw the license application, directed that "[u]pon the withdrawal or suspension of the licensing review, the NRC would begin an orderly closure of the technical review and adjudicatory activities and would document the work and insights gained from the review."[122] Accordingly, the agency requested only $10 million to "support work related to the orderly closure of the agency's Yucca Mountain licensing support activities."[123]

Two fellow NRC commissioners formally opposed the chairman's October 4 budget guidance as inconsistent with the CR.[124] Commissioner Ostendorff argued that the NRC "should continue to follow the Commission's direction in the FY2010 budget as authorized and appropriated by Congress, rather than change course as suggested in the Continuing Resolution guidance memorandum."[125] Commissioner Svinicki called the chairman's guidance "grossly premature," as the FY2011 budget request had made clear that the NRC would only begin its orderly closure of the Yucca Mountain review "upon the withdrawal or suspension of the licensing review."[126] As

---

(...continued)

"*NRC Budget Guidance*")

[118] P.L. 111-242, 111th Cong. (2010); P.L. 111-322, 111th Cong. (2010); P.L. 112-4, 112th Cong. (2011).

[119] *NRC Budget Guidance*, at 2.

[120] Letter from Gregory B. Jaczko, Chairman, Nuclear Regulatory Commission, to Congressman Joe Barton (October 27, 2010).

[121] Memorandum and Order, *In the Matter of U.S. Department of Energy*, ASLBP No. 09-892-HLW-CAB04 (February 25, 2011).

[122] Nuclear Regulatory Commission FY2011 Congressional Budget Justification, NUREG-1100 Vol. 26 (February 2010) at 95. Available at http://www.nrc.gov/reading-rm/doc-collections/nuregs/staff/sr1100/v26/sr1100v26.pdf.

[123] *Id.*

[124] In addition to the two sitting Commissioners, former Nuclear Regulatory Commission Chairman Dale E. Klein, who was a member of the Commission during the FY2011 budget discussions, also opposed the chairman's budget guidance. NRC *Chairman Klein Rebuffs Jaczko Yucca Shut-Down Alibi*, Nuclear Townhall (October 29, 2010) available at http://www.nucleartownhall.com/blog/ex-nrc-chairman-klein-rebuffs-jaczko-yucca-shut-down-alibi/.

[125] Memorandum from Commissioner William C. Ostendorff, Disagreement With Staff Budget Guidance Under Fiscal Year 2011 Continuing Resolution (October 8, 2010).

[126] Letter from Kristine L. Svinicki, Commissioner, Nuclear Regulatory Commission, to Congressman Joe Barton (November 1, 2010).

---

the license had not yet been withdrawn, Svinicki argued that any decision to terminate the license proceeding would be inconsistent with the language of the budget justification.

Congress subsequently approved the NRC's FY2011 budget proposal in passing the Full-Year Continuing Appropriations Act of 2011.[127] The measure impliedly provided the NRC, through congressional acquiescence to the NRC budget request, with the requested $10 million in funds for the "orderly closure" of the Yucca Mountain license review. Congressional approval of the NRC's FY2011 budget request, therefore, appeared to effectively sanction Chairman Jaczko's decision to begin the termination of the license review. Accordingly, Congress has likely appropriated funds to continue the shutdown of Yucca Mountain license review activities. However, debate over the validity of the chairman's budget guidance under the earlier CRs leading up to the Full-Year Continuing Appropriations Act continues.

### Analysis of Chairman Jaczko's Budget Guidance

Whether the NRC had the authority to utilize FY2011 CR funds in terminating its review of the Yucca Mountain license application remains unclear. Much of the ambiguity involved in the dispute arises from the fact that the NRC generally receives lump-sum, rather than specific, appropriations.[128] However, in determining whether the NRC appropriately used FY2011 CR funds to terminate its review of the Yucca Mountain license, two questions are raised. First, did the CR allow the NRC to follow its FY2011 budget request or was the Commission instead bound by FY2010 enacted appropriations? Second, if the NRC was bound by FY2010 enacted appropriations, could the Commission use FY2010 funds to close down the review of the Yucca Mountain license?

The CR clearly made funds available pursuant to the rates and restrictions of enacted FY2010 appropriations, unless otherwise stated, through March 18, 2011.[129] However, OMB Bulletin No. 10-03 on the apportionment of CR funds stated that "[i]f either the House or Senate has reported or passed a bill that provides no funding for an account at the time the CR is enacted, this automatic apportionment does not apply to that account."[130] The Senate reported a version of the Energy and Water appropriations bill that, though making no specific mention of the Yucca Mountain license review, could be interpreted as incorporating the NRC FY2011 budget request, which only included funds for an orderly closure of the NRC's review of the license application.[131] Thus, under the implementation guidance provided by OMB, it could be argued that the CR had not provided continued funds for the Yucca Mountain license review, as the Senate had arguably expressed an intent not to fund the license review in the future.

---

[127] P.L. 112-10, 112th Cong. (2011).

[128] Specific, or line-item, appropriations detail the amount appropriated for each purpose whereas a lump-sum appropriation covers a "number of specific programs, projects, or items." U.S. Government Accountability Office, *Principles of Federal Appropriations Law*, Vol. II: 6-5 (2006).

[129] Although the initial CR only authorized funds through December 3, 2010, it was extended to March 4, 2011, and has now been extended to March 18, 2011. P.L. 112-4, 112th Cong. (2011).

[130] Office of Management and Budget, OMB Bulletin No. 10-03, Apportionment of the Continuing Resolution(s) for Fiscal Year 2011 (September 30, 2010).

[131] S.Rept. 111-295. It is also unclear whether the Yucca Mountain license review constitutes an "account" under the OMB Apportionment Bulletin.

---

However, considering Congress had yet to expressly defund the Yucca Mountain license review, it is also possible that the NRC was obligated to follow its FY2010 enacted appropriations. Even so, the "rate for operations" and the "authority and conditions" provided in the NRC's lump-sum FY2010 enacted appropriations remain unclear.[132] Both the NRC budget request and the House report associated with the FY2010 Energy and Water Development and Related Agencies Appropriations bill contained language specifically allocating funds to "support the NRC's review of the [DOE's] licensing application to construct and operate a permanent geologic repository at Yucca Mountain."[133] The Senate report and the Conference report, on the other hand, were silent on the NRC's license review.[134] However, the Joint Explanatory Statement accompanying the Conference report expressly provides that the language of the House and Senate reports "should be complied with unless specifically addressed to the contrary in the conference report."[135] Accordingly, it could be argued that the language in the House report that expressed Congress's intent to appropriate funds for the continued review of the Yucca Mountain license was incorporated by the conference report. In contrast, Chairman Jaczko argued that "neither the text of the FY 2010 [NRC appropriation bill] and its underlying committee reports, nor the fiscal year 2011 [CR] provide the Commission with express direction on how it is to expend its appropriation ... for Yucca Mountain activities."[136] In any case, specific restrictions on lump-sum appropriations "contained in the agency's budget request or in legislative history are not legally binding on the department or agency unless they are" incorporated into the statutory language of the appropriation act.[137]

If NRC was bound by enacted FY2010 appropriations, the additional question arises of whether general principles of appropriations law allowed the NRC to use funds arguably made available to continue the licensing proceeding to instead terminate the license review. Generally speaking, agencies may use appropriated funds only for the purpose for which they were appropriated.[138] This principle has been codified in 31 U.S.C. Section 1301(a), which states: "[a]ppropriations shall be applied only to the objects for which the appropriations were made except as otherwise provided by law."[139] However, because of the nature of the lump-sum appropriation made available to the NRC, it is difficult to determine the specific purposes, if any, for which funds were appropriated. Indeed, allocating lump-sum appropriations generally lies within the discretion of the agency, as "the very point of a lump-sum appropriation is to give an agency the

---

[132] P.L. 111-85, 123 Stat. 2877-2878. The bill appropriated $1.56 billion "for necessary expenses of the Commission ..." and $10.8 million for "necessary expenses of the Office of Inspector General."

[133] Nuclear Regulatory Commission Performance Budget Fiscal Year 2010, NUREG-1100, Vol. 25 (May 2009); H.Rept. 111-203.

[134] S.Rept. 111-45; H.Rept. 111-278.

[135] H.Rept. 111-278 ("Report language included by the House which is not contradicted by the report of the Senate or the conference ... is approved by the committee of conference.")

[136] Letter from Gregory B. Jaczko, Commissioner, Nuclear Regulatory Commission, to Congressman Joe Barton (October 27, 2010).

[137] U.S. Government Accountability Office, *Principles of Federal Appropriations Law*, Vol. II: 6-6 (2006)(hereinafter *Red Book*). The Supreme Court has made clear that statements in committee reports associated with appropriations bills do not have the force of law. *See*, American Hospital Assn. v. NLRB, 499 U.S. 606 (1991); Lincoln v. Vigil, 508 U.S. 182 (1993). *See also*, LTV Aerospace Corp., 55 Comp. Gen. 307, 319 (1975) ("when Congress merely appropriates lump-sum amounts without statutorily restricting what can be done with those funds, a clear inference arises that it does not intend to impose legally binding restrictions, and indicia in committee reports and other legislative history as to how the funds should or are expected to be spent do not establish any legal requirements on federal agencies.").

[138] *Red Book*, Vol. I: 4-6 (2004).

[139] 31 U.S.C. §1301(a).

capacity to adapt to changing circumstances and meet its statutory responsibilities in what it sees as the most effective or desirable way."[140] Although legislative history and the 2010 NRC budget request may have suggested some understanding that a portion of the NRC appropriated funds would go toward funding the agency's review of the Yucca Mountain license application, there was no specific appropriation for the license review in the NRC's FY2010 appropriations.

Notwithstanding uncertainty over the specific nature of NRC appropriations, an agency generally may not use money appropriated for the implementation of a "mandatory" program to instead terminate that program.[141] In contrast, appropriated funds may be used to terminate a program if the program is not mandatory, and "the termination would not result in curtailment of the overall program to such an extent that it would no longer be consistent with the scheme of applicable program legislation."[142] The recent decision by the Board could be read as interpreting the NRC's review of the Yucca Mountain license as mandatory. For example, the Board specifically held that the NWPA "mandates progress toward a merits decision by the Nuclear Regulatory Commission."[143] Thus, the NRC's final decision on DOE's license withdrawal, and the nature of the statutory obligations created under the NWPA, will likely have an impact on whether NRC's use of funds was authorized.[144]

In response to the controversy surrounding Chairman Jaczko's budget guidance, the NRC Inspector General conducted a formal investigation into whether the chairman exceeded his authority in terminating the NRC's review of the Yucca Mountain license application.[145] The Inspector General's report concluded that the chairman's actions were supported by the NRC general counsel and consistent with the chairman's budget execution authority; OMB guidance; the Administration's decision to terminate the Yucca Mountain project; and the NRC's FY2011 budget policy decisions.[146] However, the Inspector General also concluded that the chairman was not "forthcoming" with all Commissioners with respect to the breadth of the close-out

---

[140] Lincoln v. Vigil, 508 U.S. 182, 192 (1993).

[141] *Red Book*, Vol. I: 4-17-18 (2004).

[142] *Id.*

[143] Memorandum and Order, *In the Matter of U.S. Department of Energy*, ASLBP No. 09-892-HLW-CAB04 (June 29, 2010).

[144] A similar factual scenario from the late 1970s and early 1980s suggests that congressional intent plays an integral role in determining whether an agency can use appropriated funds to terminate a program. Congress authorized the design, construction, and operation of the Clinch River Breeder Reactor in 1970. Until FY1983, the program had been funded as part of a lump sum appropriation, although "amounts intended for the project [had] been indicated in committee reports accompanying the appropriation act." On three instances during this period the Comptroller General denied requests from DOE's predecessor, the Energy Research and Development Administration (ERDA),to use appropriated funds to terminate the program. Congress's position on the project "changed substantially," however, in FY1994. Legislative history reflected that no funds were designated for the project and a continuing resolution directed that DOE not "undertake any new activities relating" to the reactor. Following passage of the continuing resolution, DOE again requested authority to use previously appropriated funds to terminate the reactor project. Noting that "the funding situation was very different at the time we issued our earlier decision," the Comptroller General determined that DOE was not "unreasonable in concluding that further funding for the project [was] not likely to be forthcoming. We think this provides the Department with a legal basis for terminating the project." Government Accountability Office, Decisions of the Comptroller General, 63 Comp. Gen. 75 (1983). See also, *Red Book* Vol. I 4-18 (2004).

[145] *NRC IG Report*, *supra* note 111.

[146] *Id.* at 2.

activities.[147] The report found that the chairman had "strategically provided three of the four commissioners with varying amounts of information about his intention to proceed to closure."[148]

## NRC Suspends Licensing Proceedings

The described budget dispute notwithstanding, with only four commissioners eligible to vote and the Commission apparently at an impasse, the NRC released an order on September 9, 2011, stating that the "Commission finds itself evenly divided on whether to take the affirmative action of overturning or upholding the Board's decision."[149] Although not reaching a decision on the license withdrawal, the order, citing "budgetary limitations," directed the Board to "complete all necessary and appropriate case management activities, including disposal of all matters currently pending before it and comprehensively documenting the full history of the adjudicatory proceeding," by the end of the fiscal year.[150] On September 30, 2011, the Board officially announced that "because both future appropriated [Nuclear Waste Fund] dollars and [Full-Time Equivalent positions] for this proceeding are uncertain, and consistent with the Commission's Memorandum and order of September 9, 2011, this proceeding is suspended."[151]

It is important to note that the Yucca Mountain proceedings were terminated by the NRC as a budgetary matter. The proceedings were not terminated by actions of DOE or the Obama Administration. Indeed, the Yucca Mountain license has not been withdrawn. Upon suspending the proceedings, the Board made clear that because the Commission remained evenly divided, "the Board's decision to deny DOE's motion to withdraw [the license], therefore stands."[152]

## D.C. Circuit Litigation

### DOE's License Withdrawal

In conjunction with opposing DOE's motion for withdrawal at the administrative level, a number of parties have filed cases in federal court in an attempt to stop DOE and the Obama Administration from terminating the Yucca Mountain program.[153] These statutory claims, filed by

---

[147] *Id.* at 44.

[148] *Id.*

[149] Order of the Nuclear Regulatory Commission, *In the Matter of U.S. Department of Energy*, No. 63-001-HLW (September 9, 2011).

[150] *Id.*

[151] Memorandum and Order, *In the Matter of U.S. Department of Energy*, ASLBP No. 09-892-HLW-CAB04, (September 30, 2011). The Board also noted that "[a]lthough we have been informed that the agency has current appropriated Fiscal Year 2011 Nuclear Waste Funds that could be carried over into the next fiscal year, there are no Full-Time Equivalent positions (i.e., federal employee positions) requested in the President's Fiscal Year 2012 Budget for Yucca Mountain High-Level Waste activities." *Id.*

[152] *Id.*

[153] In a related suit, New York, Connecticut, and Vermont challenged the NRC's "waste confidence" determination in a complaint filed with the D.C. Circuit on February 14, 2011. In September 2010, the NRC approved a revision to the agency's waste confidence rule, affirming NRC's confidence that "spent fuel generated in any reactor can be stored safely and without significant environmental impacts for at least 60 years beyond the licensed life for operation ... of that reactor ..." 10 C.F.R. §51.23. The previous rule only expressed confidence that nuclear waste could be stored for "30 years beyond the licensed life for operation" of any reactor. 10 C.F.R. §51.23 (2009) Additionally, whereas the previous rule stated that "the Commission believes there is reasonable assurance that at least one mined geologic repository will be available within the first quarter of the twenty-first century, and sufficient repository capacity will be (continued...)

---

South Carolina, Washington, and other private plaintiffs, have been consolidated in the D.C. Circuit.[154] The states of South Carolina and Washington have played significant roles in much of the litigation surrounding the Yucca Mountain facility. DOE's Hanford Nuclear Reservation, located in southeast Washington, is currently home to approximately 53 million gallons of defense-related nuclear waste—a majority of which was to be disposed of, after solidification, in the future Yucca Mountain repository.[155] Similarly, DOE's Savannah River Site is home to large amounts of high-level waste. The parties have asked the court to block DOE from withdrawing the Yucca Mountain license.

The complaints filed in the case[156] allege violations of the NWPA, the National Environmental Policy Act and the Administrative Procedure Act—claims similar to those made before the NRC. The petitioners assert that the NWPA creates a mandatory obligation on behalf of the Secretary to submit the application, as well as a mandatory obligation on behalf of the NRC to review the application.[157] Any withdrawal, the complaints argue, would be in violation of the site selection provisions of the NWPA. Petitioners also argue that DOE's decision to abandon the Yucca Mountain facility violates NEPA. NEPA mandates that any federal agency prepare an assessment of the potential environmental impact before proceeding with a "major federal action significantly affecting the quality of the human environment."[158] Petitioners argue that any decision to close Yucca Mountain must be preceded by a NEPA assessment or an explanation of why the agency action will not have a significant impact on the environment. Finally, petitioners argue that the decision to terminate the Yucca Mountain project after decades of progress without articulating "any explanation for its decision that rationally ties its choice to any specific facts" is arbitrary and capricious under the APA and therefore unlawful.[159]

The D.C. Circuit initially granted the petitioners' request to expedite the proceedings, invited the parties to file briefs, and scheduled oral argument for September 23, 2010.[160] The circuit court's decision to hear the claims before the NRC had completed its proceedings was unusual, as previously noted, considering principles of judicial economy, finality, and exhaustion. Shortly thereafter, however, the D.C. Circuit, on a motion from the Department of Justice (DOJ), reversed course and ordered that the "cases be held in abeyance pending further proceedings before the [NRC]."[161] Specifically, the circuit court directed the parties to await the NRC's "final decision in its pending review of the Licensing Board's June 29, 2010, decision."[162] However, after months

---

(...continued)

available within 30 years beyond the licensed life for operation of any reactor...," the revised rule states only that "the Commission believes there is reasonable assurance that sufficient mined geologic repository capacity will be available to dispose of the commercial high-level radioactive waste and spent fuel generated in any reactor when necessary." *Compare* 10 C.F.R. §51.23 (2009) *with* 10 C.F.R. §51.23 (2011).

[154] *See*, In re Aiken County, 645 F.3d 428 (D.C. Cir. 2011).

[155] State of Washington's Petition for Leave to Intervene and Request for Hearing, *In the Matter of U.S. Department of Energy*, ASLBP NO. 09-892-HLW-CAB04, March 3, 2010.

[156] *Id.* at 4. The U.S. Courts of Appeals have original jurisdiction over challenges to agency action under the NWPA. NWPA §119.

[157] State of Washington's Petition for Leave to Intervene and Request for Hearing, *In the Matter of U.S. Department of Energy*, ASLBP NO. 09-892-HLW-CAB04 (March 3, 2010) at 10-11.

[158] 42 U.S.C. §4332.

[159] *See, e.g.,* Motion for Preliminary Injunction, Washington v. DOE, No-10-1050 (D.C. Cir. April 13, 2010).

[160] Order, *In re Aiken County*, No. 10-1050 (D.C. Cir. May 3, 2010).

[161] Order, *In re Aiken County*, No. 10-1050 (D.C. Cir. July 28, 2010).

[162] *Id.*

---

of delays, additional controversy,[163] and no final decision from the NRC, the D.C. Circuit lifted the stay on December 10, 2010, and again agreed to expedite the cases.[164]

## *In re Aiken County*

In a unanimous decision, the D.C. Circuit dismissed the parties' claims on July 1, 2011—determining as a threshold matter that the "challenges to the ongoing administrative process are premature."[165] Consequently, the court did not reach the merits of the issue. First, the court held that the petitioners' challenge to DOE's attempt to withdraw the Yucca Mountain license application was not yet ripe for review and therefore not within the court's jurisdiction.[166] Ripeness is a justiciability doctrine adopted "to prevent the courts, through avoidance of premature adjudication, from entangling themselves in abstract disagreements over administrative policies, and also to protect the agencies from judicial interference until an administrative decision has been formalized and its effects felt in a concrete way by the challenging parties."[167] The court determined that the potential license withdrawal was based on "contingent" future events, as the NRC's review of the Board's decision and the Board's review of the Yucca Mountain license remain "ongoing."[168] In addition, a decision from either body could very well resolve the petitioners' claims in the near future.[169] Thus, the court reasoned that until the Board either grants or denies the license application, or the NRC reaches a decision overturning the Board's decision denying the license withdrawal, there is no concrete agency action to challenge.

Moreover, the D.C. Circuit held that the petitioners' challenge to the Administration's decision to "unilaterally and irrevocably terminate the Yucca Mountain repository process" was "simply not reviewable by this court."[170] The court determined that DOE's "publicly stated desire and intention to abandon the Yucca Mountain repository" did not constitute final agency action as required for judicial review under the Administrative Procedure Act.[171] Additionally, the APA provides for review of an agency's failure to act only where a "plaintiff asserts that an agency failed to take a *discrete* agency action that it is *required to take*."[172] The court determined that DOE had not yet failed to take an action it was required to take, and given the lack of finality in the administrative process, review of any proposed decision to abandon the Yucca Mountain facility was premature.

---

[163] The D.C. Circuit's order lifting the stay on the Yucca Mountain cases came shortly after the NRC announced it would be terminating its review of the Yucca Mountain license application.

[164] Order, *In re Aiken County*, No. 10-1050 (D.C. Cir. December 10, 2010).

[165] In re Aiken County, 645 F.3d 428, 438 (D.C. Cir. 2011).

[166] *Id.* at 434.

[167] *Id.* at 433 (*citing* Abbott Labs v. Gardner, 387 U.S. 136, 148-49 (1967).

[168] *Id.* at 438.

[169] *Id.* at 435 ("Between the [NRC's] possible review of the denial order and the [Board's] consideration of the Yucca Mountain license application, the only administrative outcome that will fail to resolve the issues presented in Petitioner's first claim would be if the Commission reviews and overturns the [Board's] denial, permitting the DOE to withdraw its license application. At that point, petitioners would have the opportunity to demonstrate whether the effects of the DOE action are 'felt in a concrete way by the challenging parties.") (citations omitted).

[170] *Id.* at 436.

[171] *Id.* at 437.

[172] *Id.* at 437 (*citing* Norton v. S. Utah Wilderness Alliance, 542 U.S. 55, 64 (2004)(emphasis in original)).

---

Although the D.C. Circuit dismissed the petitioner's claims—claims that focused primarily on the actions of the President and DOE[173]—the opinion will likely have two significant consequences on future NRC actions. First, the opinion noted that continued delay by NRC in reaching a decision on the license withdrawal would not "insulate" the agency's inaction from judicial review. Thus, the court noted that should the NRC fail to act within the express three-year time frame established under the NWPA,[174] then the petitioners would have a new cause of action to "compel" agency action "unreasonably delayed."[175] Although not setting a specific date beyond which the NRC would be in violation of the NWPA, the court did note that regardless of whether the three-year review period was measured from the date the license application was submitted or the date it was docketed, "in either case, the deadline for the [NRC] to act is at hand."[176] Accordingly, if NRC does not take action on the Yucca Mountain license in the near future, the D.C. Circuit seems willing and able to reconsider the issue.

Second, the opinion expressly stated that NRC "maintains a statutory duty" to continue the review of the Yucca Mountain license application.[177] Although the court took notice of the fact that petitioners had pointed "to evidence that the [NRC] has suspended the [Board's] review," the court clearly stated that "the NWPA requires the [NRC] to review the application, and therefore we must assume that the [NRC] will comply with its statutory mandate."[178] As will be discussed in the next section, NRC Chairman Gregory Jaczko has indeed already taken significant steps to terminate all NRC license review activities. Such action could reasonably be characterized as contrary to the D.C. Circuit's interpretation of the NWPA.

## *Litigation Focus Shifts from DOE to NRC*

Perhaps recognizing the D.C. Circuit's focus on the statutory obligations of NRC rather than DOE, the plaintiffs promptly filed new claims against the NRC—arguing that the agency had "unreasonably delayed consideration of the license application." The petition asked the D.C. Circuit to compel NRC to issue a "final decision" on the license "within 30 days."[179] Oral arguments in the case were heard on May 2, 2012, and focused mainly on the consequences of the appeals court ordering the NRC to resume its review of the license application, and whether the NRC's justification for the shutdown of the license review was based on policy considerations or budgetary restraints.[180] Also on May 2, the court invited the Department of Justice to submit a

---

[173] In a concurring opinion, Judge Brown noted that the petitioners' focus on the President and DOE may have been counterproductive: "It is arguable the NRC has abdicated its statutory responsibility under the NWPA.... Despite months of extensive briefing and protracted questioning at oral argument, Petitioners still see only the President and his administration obstructing their path to judicial review.... Such stubbornness may snatch defeat from the jaws of victory." *Id.* at 438 (Brown, J., concurring). Judge Kavanaugh also issued a concurring opinion that focused on presidential control of the executive branch and highlighted that fact that the existing statutory framework gives the NRC, rather than the President, "the final word in the Executive Branch on whether the Executive Branch may terminate the Yucca Mountain project." *Id.* at 439 (Kavanaugh, J., concurring).

[174] The NWPA states that, absent an extension, "the [NRC] shall issue a final decision approving or disapproving the issuance of a construction authorization not later than the expiration of 3 years after the date of the submission of such application...." NWPA §114(d).

[175] In re Aiken County, 645 F.3d 428, 436 (D.C. Cir. 2011).

[176] *Id.* at 436.

[177] *Id.* at 437. The language would likely qualify as dicta as it was not necessary to the ultimate holding.

[178] *Id.* at 435.

[179] Brief of Petitioners, In re Aiken County, No. 11-1271 (D.C. Cir. December 5, 2011) at 54.

[180] The D.C. Circuit was reportedly "skeptical" of the NRC's position, and gave the agency's arguments a "cool (continued...)

---

brief "expressing the views of the United States on whether this court should issue a writ of mandamus ordering the [NRC] to act on the [DOE's] pending Yucca Mountain license application."[181] Because NRC is an independent agency with limited independent litigating authority, the DOJ has not been managing the agency's legal defense as is typically the case for litigation involving executive agencies.[182]

## Suspending the Nuclear Waste Fund Fee

Shortly after the D.C. Circuit lifted its stay on the license withdrawal claims, the court also dismissed a Yucca Mountain-related case brought by the National Association of Regulatory Commissioners (NARUC) and the Nuclear Energy Institute (NEI).[183] NARUC and NEI had filed a claim asking the court to order Secretary Chu to conduct the required annual assessment of the Nuclear Waste Fund fee and suspend collection of the fee pending that assessment.[184] Nuclear power providers have collectively paid approximately $750 million per year in fees to the fund, which currently has an approximate balance of $24 billion.

Under the NWPA, DOE was authorized to enter into contracts with nuclear power providers to gather and dispose of nuclear waste in exchange for payments by the providers into the statutorily established Nuclear Waste Fund (NWF).[185] However, the Secretary is required to "annually review" the adequacy of the fee to ensure it provides "sufficient revenues to offset costs" incurred as a result of nuclear waste disposal activities.[186] If the Secretary finds that "insufficient or excess revenues are being collected … the Secretary shall propose an adjustment to the fee to insure (sic) full cost recovery."[187] At the time the claim was filed, DOE had not conducted a fee assessment since FY2008. NARUC and NEI argued that given the Administration's attempts to terminate the Yucca Mountain facility, "there is no current basis to judge the adequacy of the fee to cover future costs because the method of disposal and its life-cycle costs are unknown."[188] Thus, Congress intended that "[i]f no fee can be justified based on record evidence, no fee can be charged."[189] However, DOE subsequently released its most recent assessment of the NWF fee and the court dismissed the claim as moot, but suggested that the parties could challenge the new fee assessment,[190] which they did.

---

(...continued)

reception." *See*, Alan Kovski, *Judges Skeptical of Justification for Halt of NRC Action on Yucca Mountain License*, BNA Daily Report for Executives, May 3, 2012.

[181] Order, *In re Aiken County*, No. 11-1271 (D.C. Cir., May 2, 2012).

[182] The NRC is granted limited independent litigating authority under 28 U.S.C. §2348.

[183] National Association of Regulatory Utility Commissioners v. DOE, 2010 U.S. App. LEXIS 25579 (D.C. Cir. December 13, 2010).

[184] *Id.*

[185] *See*, CRS Report R40996, *Contract Liability Arising from the Nuclear Waste Policy Act (NWPA) of 1982*, by Todd Garvey.

[186] NWPA §302(a)(4).

[187] *Id.*

[188] Final Initial Brief of Petitioner, National Association of Regulatory Commissioners v. DOE, No. 10-1074 (D.C. Cir. October 18, 2010) at 7.

[189] *Id.* at 15.

[190] National Association of Regulatory Utility Commissioners v. DOE, 2010 U.S. App. LEXIS 25579 (D.C. Cir. December 13, 2010). The parties refiled their claims challenging the new fee adequacy assessment. These claims are currently pending before the D.C. Circuit. National Association of Regulatory Commissioners v. DOE, Nos. 11-1066, (continued...)

---

On June 1, 2012, the D.C. Circuit issued an opinion holding that DOE had "failed to perform a valid evaluation" as required by the NWPA.[191] Although reserving its power to do so, the court was not willing to order the Secretary to suspend the collection of the NWF fee.[192] Instead, the court declared the Secretary's evaluation of the necessity of the fee to be "legally defective" and remanded the case to DOE to reevaluate its fee assessment consistent with the court's opinion.[193]

# Congressional Reaction to Proposed Termination of the Yucca Mountain Facility

Congress has been relatively active in response to the Obama Administration's proposed termination of Yucca Mountain, DOE's motion to withdraw the license application, and the NRC's decision to cease review of the license application. Congress has not, however, restored funding for the Yucca Mountain facility or the NRC's review of the Yucca Mountain license. Although no funds have been appropriated, the House of Representatives has attempted to utilize appropriations to prevent the termination of the Yucca Mountain program. For example, the House passed an appropriations bill on July 15, 2011, that would have restored funding for the Yucca Mountain repository by providing $25 million to DOE to "carry out the purposes of the Nuclear Waste Policy Act" and $20 million to the NRC to "continue the Yucca Mountain license application."[194] The bill would also have expressly prohibited appropriated funds from being used to "conduct closure of adjudicatory functions, technical review, or support activities associated with the Yucca Mountain geologic repository license application until the Nuclear Regulatory Commission reverses [the Board's decision], or for actions that irrevocably remove the possibility that Yucca Mountain may be a repository option in the future."[195]

The Senate, however, did not provide any funds for the program.[196] In conference, the funding was removed, but language was included in the Joint Explanatory Statement of the conference report[197] that directed DOE to continue to work toward developing a solution for nuclear waste disposal. To that end, the conference report directed DOE to "develop a strategy for the management of spent nuclear fuel and other nuclear waste within 6 months" of the publication of

---

(...continued)

11-1068 (D.C. Cir. 2011).

[191] National Association of Regulatory Utility Commissioners v. DOE, 2012 U.S. App. LEXIS 11044, 2 (D.C. Cir. June 1, 2012).

[192] *Id.* at 18 ("[W]e think our authority to review the Secretary's 2010 determination under the Administrative Procedure Act includes the power to direct the Secretary to suspend the fee. But it is premature to do so now. It is appropriate for us simply to declare that the Secretary's determination is legally defective and to remand.").

[193] The appeals court ordered DOE to "respond to the remand within six months." *Id.* at 19.

[194] H.R. 2354 112th Cong. (2011).

[195] *Id.* at §604.

[196] S.Rept. 112-75, at 96 (2011) ("The Committee recommends no funding for the nuclear waste disposal program.").

[197] *Id.* As part of the Joint Explanatory Statement, as opposed to the text of the appropriations bill, it is unlikely that these provisions would be considered legally binding. *See,* American Hospital Assn. v. NLRB, 499 U.S. 606 (1991); Lincoln v. Vigil, 508 U.S. 182 (1993). *See also,* LTV Aerospace Corp., 55 Comp. Gen. 307, 319 (1975) ("when Congress merely appropriates lump-sum amounts without statutorily restricting what can be done with those funds, a clear inference arises that it does not intend to impose legally binding restrictions, and indicia in committee reports and other legislative history as to how the funds should or are expected to be spent do not establish any legal requirements on federal agencies.").

---

the Blue Ribbon Commission's final report.[198] Additionally, the report stated that because "multiple geologic repositories will ultimately be required for the long-term disposition of the nation's spent fuel and nuclear waste," DOE was directed to "focus, within available funds, $3,000,000 on development of models for potential partnerships to manage spent nuclear fuel and high level waste, and $7,000,000 on characterization of potential geologic repository media."[199] The report also directed DOE to "preserve all documentation relating to Yucca Mountain, including technical information, records, and other documents, as well as scientific data and physical materials."[200]

FY2013 appropriations appear to be unfolding in a similar manner. The House Appropriations Committee has approved an appropriations bill that would provide $25 million to DOE to proceed with the license application and direct the NRC to utilize "prior-year funds to complete the Yucca Mountain license application."[201] The version approved by the Senate Appririations Committee does not include similar funding, but rather directs DOE to establish a pilot program to operate "at least one consolidated storage facility for spent nuclear fuel."[202]

The NRC's delay in coming to a final decision on DOE's motion to withdraw the Yucca Mountain license application and the agency's decision to halt the license review have also generated a significant congressional response. Much of the criticism of the NRC has focused on Chairman Jaczko. For example, the majority staff of the House Oversight and Government Reform Committee conducted an investigation into NRC decision making and found that "the Chairman's interpretation of his authority evolved to closely resemble that of a single administrator—his management style and aggressive behavior simultaneously eroded the collegial structure and values inherent in the NRC."[203]

The then-ranking Members of the House Select Committee on Energy Independence and Global Warming, House Energy and Commerce Committee, House Science and Technology Committee, and House Natural Resources Committee expressed their concern over Chairman Jaczko's decision to "unilaterally" halt the NRC's review of the Yucca Mountain license in a public letter to the Commission.[204] The letter called Chairman Jaczko's decision to base budget guidance on the FY2011 budget request rather than enacted FY2010 appropriations "suspect."[205] The then-ranking Member of the House Appropriations Committee as well as six members of the House Appropriations Subcommittee on Energy and Water Development—the Subcommittee that controls DOE and NRC appropriations—told Chairman Jaczko that his actions "may seriously

---

[198] *Id*. at 850. The report was issued on January 26, 2012.

[199] *Id*. at 850-51. The Joint Explanatory Statement also included $10 million to "expand [DOE's] capabilities for assessing issues related to the aging and safety of storing spent nuclear fuel…" *Id*. at 851.

[200] *Id*.

[201] H.Rept. 112-462, 112th Cong. (2012) at 108, 172. The bill also provides that "[n]one of the funds made available in this Act may be used to conduct closure of adjudicatory functions, technical review, or support activities associated with the Yucca Mountain geologic repository license application, or for actions that irrevocably remove the possibility that Yucca Mountain may be a repository option in the future." H.R. 5325 §508, 112th Cong. (2012).

[202] S.Rept. 112-164, 112th Cong. (2012) at 78.

[203] Majority Staff Report, Committee on Oversight and Government Reform, *A Crisis of Leadership: How the Actions of Chairman Gregory Jaczko Are Damaging the Nuclear Regulatory Commission* (December 13, 2011) at 4-5. *Available at* http://oversight.house.gov/images/stories/Reports/12-13-11%20NRC%20Report%20Final%201.pdf.

[204] Letter from Rep. Jim Sensenbrenner *et al.* to Gregory Jaczko, Commissioner, Nuclear Regulatory Commission (October 13, 2010).

[205] *Id*.

erode the NRC's relationship with this subcommittee."[206] In a strongly worded letter, the Members threatened increased oversight of the NRC, concluding with the warning: "If you continue to shut down the Yucca Mountain license application, which can only be seen as a partisan act, we will reconsider the flexibilities which the NRC has long enjoyed due to its reputation as an independent body."[207]

Other Members of Congress asked the Inspector General of the NRC to "convene a formal investigation into the Chairman's recent actions to shut down the project."[208] As noted previously, the NRC Inspector General released his official report on June 6, 2011.[209] The scope of the investigation included a consideration of the chairman's decision to terminate all Yucca Mountain license review activities; the delay in the NRC's review of the Board's decision on DOE's authority to withdraw the Yucca Mountain license application; and the "impact the Chairman's management style has on the collegial functioning of the NRC Commission."[210] The report did not find that the chairman had violated any laws or acted illegally in any way. The report concluded that the chairman's direction to NRC staff to begin closure of the Yucca Mountain license review was within his authority and that the chairman has not improperly delayed a final NRC decision on the DOE license withdrawal. However, the report did make clear that the chairman had acted to "strategically" control information distribution to the both the other Commissioners and the NRC staff.[211] The report noted that "because [the Commissioner] acts as the gatekeeper to determine what is a policy matter versus an administrative manner, and manages and controls information available to the other commissioners, they are uncertain as to whether they are adequately informed of policy matters that should be brought to their attention."[212]

Presumably as a result of the controversy surrounding Chairman Jaczko's leadership at the NRC, the Consolidated Appropriations Act of 2012 contained an express statutory provision prohibiting the chairman of NRC from terminating "any program, project, or activity without the approval of a majority vote of the Commissioners of the [NRC] approving such action."[213]

Additionally, the 112th Congress has held a number of hearings that have focused on the current Yucca Mountain controversy.[214] For example, the Senate Committee on Energy and Natural Resources and the House Energy and Commerce Committee held hearings on the BRC's final report. Additionally, the House Oversight and Government Reform Committee, the House Energy

---

[206] Letter from Rep. Jerry Lewis to Gregory Jaczko, Commissioner, Nuclear Regulatory Commission (October 20, 2010).

[207] *Id.*

[208] Letter from Congressman Fred Upton and Congressman Ed Whitfield to Hubert T. Bell, Inspector General, Nuclear Regulatory Commission (October 19, 2010).

[209] *NRC IG Report, supra* note 111.

[210] *Id.* at 2.

[211] *Id.* at 44.

[212] *Id.* at 45-46.

[213] P.L. 112-74, 112th Cong. §401 (2011).

[214] In addition, the majority staff of the House Science, Space and Technology Committee released a lengthy report entitled *Yucca Mountain: The Administration's Impact on U.S. Nuclear Waste Management Policy* that was critical of the Administration's policy shift. *Available at* http://science.house.gov/sites/republicans.science.house.gov/files/documents/Letters/Yucca%20Mountain%20-%20The%20Administration%27s%20Impact%20on%20U.S.%20Nuclear%20Waste%20Management%20Policy%20FULL.pdf.

---

and Commerce Subcommittee on Environment and the Economy and the Subcommittee on Energy and Power, and the Senate Environment and Public Works Committee have held a series of hearings on the Yucca Mountain program, the NRC's shutdown of the license review, the finding of the NRC Inspector General report, or NRC staff perspectives on recent NRC actions.[215] These hearings, in conjunction with the findings of the NRC Inspector General report, have generally portrayed an internal environment at the NRC in which some Commissioners and staff have been frustrated by many of the actions taken by Commissioner Jaczko, and appear to be discouraged by the chairman's allegedly unilateral decision-making process.[216]

Although much of the resistance to the shutdown has come from the South Carolina and Washington delegations, a growing number of Members have expressed their opposition to the Obama Administration's plans. In July 2010, 91 Members of Congress signed a letter to Secretary Chu asking that DOE "halt all actions to dismantle operations at Yucca Mountain" until the NRC and the D.C. Circuit resolve the license dispute.[217] The letter made clear the Members' position that DOE had "overstepped its bounds" and "ignored congressional intent" in attempting to terminate the Yucca Mountain facility.[218]

Finally, resolutions have been introduced in the House that would express support for Yucca Mountain as the "nation's primary permanent nuclear waste storage site;"[219] express disapproval of the DOE motion to withdraw the Yucca Mountain license application;[220] and condemn the NRC's decision to halt its review of the Yucca Mountain license application.[221] A Resolution of Inquiry has also been introduced that would ask the President and Secretary of Energy to provide the House of Representatives with documents relating to the proposed termination of the Yucca Mountain program.[222] Other bills have also been introduced that would limit DOE's ability to collect NWF fees.[223]

For a description of other legislative proposals pertaining to the Yucca Mountain project and the NWPA, see CRS Report RL33461, *Civilian Nuclear Waste Disposal*, by Mark Holt.

---

[215] The Role of the Nuclear Regulatory Commission in America's Energy Future: Hearing Before the H. Subcommittee on Energy and Power and the Subcommittee on Environment and the Economy, 112th Cong. (May 4, 2011); The NRC Inspector General Report on the "NRC Chairman's Unilateral Decision to Terminate NRC's Review of the DOE Yucca Mountain Repository License Application": Hearing Before the H. Subcommittee on Environment and the Economy, 112th Cong. (June 14, 2011); NRC Repository Safety Division, Staff Perspective on Yucca License Review: Hearing Before the H. Subcommittee on Environment and the Economy, 112th Cong. (June 24, 2011).

[216] This portrayal was buttressed by a letter sent to White House Chief of Staff William Daley, in which NRC Commissioners Svinicki, Apostolakis, Magwood, and Ostendorff expressed "grave concerns regarding the leadership and management practices exercised by [NRC] Chairman Gregory Jaczko." The letter asserted that the chairman's conduct—alleged to include intimidating and bullying senior staff, ignoring the will of the majority of the Commission, and interacting with fellow Commissioners with "intemperance and disrespect"—was causing "serious damage to the institution" and impairing the "effective execution of the agency's mission." Letter from NRC Commissioners Kristine Svinicki, George Apostolakis, William Magwood IV, and William Ostendorff to William Daley, White House Chief of Staff (October 13, 2011).

[217] Letter from Sen. Patty Murray *et al.* to Stephen Chu, Secretary of Energy (July 6, 2010).

[218] *Id.*

[219] H.Res. 1123 111th Cong. (2010).

[220] H.Res. 1209 111th Cong. (2010).

[221] H.Res. 1732 111th Cong. (2010).

[222] H.Res. 1466 111th Cong. (2010).

[223] H.R. 2372 111th Cong. (2010); S. 861 111th Cong. (2010).

# The Future of Yucca Mountain

While the result of the ongoing dispute over the attempted termination of the Yucca Mountain program remains uncertain, continued opposition to the proposed termination in the House of Representatives will likely have a significant impact on the ultimate fate of the program. A number of leading House Republicans have voiced strong opposition to abandoning the Yucca Mountain repository. For example, the chairmen of a number of influential committees—including the House Budget Committee, House Committee on Appropriations, House Committee on Appropriations Subcommittee on Energy and Water, House Natural Resources Committee, and House Committee on Science, Space, and Technology—have all opposed the Administration's attempts to terminate the Yucca Mountain project. Additionally, Representative Darrell Issa, chairman of the House Committee on Oversight and Government Reform, opposes the Administration's position on Yucca Mountain.[224] Speaker of the House John Boehner has also indicated his interest in reviving the Yucca Mountain program, arguing that "[w]e've invested tens of billions of dollars in a storage facility that's as safe as anything we're going to find."[225] Consequently, the Yucca Mountain dispute will not only unfold legally before the NRC and in the D.C. Circuit, but also politically in the form of likely appropriations disputes, investigations, and oversight hearings.

Moreover, changes in the makeup of the NRC may also have a significant impact on the future of Yucca Mountain. After a tumultuous three years as chairman, Gregory Jaczko submitted his resignation as chairman of the NRC on May 21, 2012, "effective upon the confirmation of my successor."[226] President Obama subsequently nominated Allison Macfarlane, former member of the Blue Ribbon Commission and an associate professor of environmental science and policy at George Mason University, to succeed Jaczko as chairman. Macfarlane is known as a critic of the Yucca Mountain facility.[227] The Senate is expected to hold a joint confirmation hearing on the nomination of Macfarlane and the renomination of Commissioner Svinicki.

## Author Contact Information

Todd Garvey
Legislative Attorney
tgarvey@crs.loc.gov, 7-0174

---

[224] *See*, Rep. Darrell Issa, *Nuclear Power and Our Energy Future*, The San Diego Union-Tribune (April 18, 2010) ("Despite a commitment for increasing loan guarantees to ramp up the development of new nuclear plants, the administration's determination to shutter the proposed nuclear waste repository at Yucca Mountain effectively jeopardizes this goal.").

[225] Statement by Rep. John Boehner to the City Club of Cleveland (August 24, 2010).

[226] See, Statement of NRC Chairman Gregory B. Jaczko, May 21, 2012, available at http://pbadupws nrc.gov/docs/ML1214/ ML12142 A168.pdf

[227] *See, e.g.,* Lynn Garner, "Obama Nominates Yucca Mountain Opponent to Lead Nuclear Regulatory Commission," BNA Daily Environment Report, May 25, 2012 (reporting that Macfarlane did not object to being called a "Yucca critic.").